for mom and dad,
from Bruce & Leslie
christmas 1993

The Coasts of India

The Coasts of India

With 80 Photographs and Captions
by ASHVIN MEHTA

Introduction by Andrew Robinson

THAMES AND HUDSON

Photographs and captions © 1987 Ashvin Mehta
Introduction © 1987 Thames and Hudson Ltd, London

First published in the United States in 1987 by
Thames and Hudson Inc., 500 Fifth Avenue,
New York, New York 10110

Library of Congress Catalog Card Number 87-50202

Printed and bound in Japan by Dai Nippon Printing, Tokyo

Introduction

In the last century or so the face of India has been said to be turned in on itself, or towards the Himalayas, or towards the West or Russia or China; seldom if ever towards the Indian Ocean which surrounds much of the subcontinent. This is a paradox which becomes even more surprising when one considers that Indian seafaring appears to date back to the time of Babylon and certainly to before the birth of Christ. By the time of Marco Polo, Indians were established all over the lands around the Indian Ocean. Within India today, five of her greatest monuments stand beside the ocean: the cave sculptures at Elephanta near Bombay, the Siva temple at Rameshwaram near Cape Comorin, the rock-cut sculptures and temples at Mahabalipuram near Madras, the Sun Temple at Konarak, and the Jagannath Temple at Puri. Also, two of her four great cities, Bombay and Madras, are maritime, and a third, Calcutta, was a great port, the second city of the British Empire, for much of its history. They were founded, of course, by Europeans, who were the first invaders of India to come from the sea, as far as we know.

This fact may be a clue to the paradox. Rabindranath Tagore, the national poet of India, who grew up in Calcutta in the 1870s and 1880s at the noonday of imperial splendour, certainly felt so:

> The history of the Northmen of Europe is resonant with the music of the sea. That sea is not merely topographical in its significance, but represents certain ideals of life which still guide the history and inspire the creations of that race. In the sea, nature presented herself to those men in her aspect of danger, a barrier which seemed to be at constant war with the land and its children. The sea was the challenge of untamed nature to the indomitable human soul. And man did not flinch; he fought and won, and the spirit of fight continued in him.

Such a people, Tagore went on

> find delight in turning by force the antagonism of circumstances into obedience. Truth appears to them in her aspect of dualism, the perpetual conflict of good and evil, which has no reconciliation, which can only end in victory or defeat.

The Indian ideal, he felt, lay in a harmony with natural forces, nurtured by the level forest tracts of northern India, not by the exciting rapacity of the sea.

This poetic contrast finds its unique physical expression at the southern tip of India, Cape Comorin, where the Bay of Bengal and the Arabian Sea merge, blue and green, with the Indian Ocean: Kanya Kumari as Indians know it, which means 'Virgin Princess'. A temple dedicated to her stands at the tip. She is Siva's consort but her wedding never took place. The other gods feared for their power and sent Indra in the guise of a rooster to crow in the path of the groom's wedding party, who thought the auspicious moment had passed and returned to the palace.

'Her numinous beauty is unclouded even by the fact that the Belgian nuns who have their convent less than a mile from the temple have called her "Kanya Mary",' writes the entertaining and extraordinary Aghenanda Bharati, a Hindu monk of Austrian birth now settled in the United States. 'The sacred, fragrant air that pervades Dravidian shrines – a blend of incense, austerely reticent bats, old sandstone and continuous worship through the centuries, wild coconuts, plantains, flowers, and deep piety – is more fragrant and thicker here, for it is enriched by the humidity of the ocean.'

Even for the non-Hindu, Kanya Kumari is a place with special powers to induce contemplation. From the shore you watch the shifting colours of the waters and, at sunrise, the dark glittering expanse of ocean dotted with shark-like silhouettes of one-man fishing rigs out before light. From a large rock off-shore, to which you are taken by launch, you see a less placid face. It was to here that the itinerant apostle of muscular Hinduism, Swami Vivekananda, swam in a state of mental turbulence some time in the winter of 1892 and meditated for three nights before swimming back to Kanya Kumari, avoiding the sharks. His experience on the rock launched him on his first, meteoric passage to the West, intially to the United States in 1893 (where he proved irresistible to the ladies of Chicago and the still fairly Wild West), and eventually led to his founding the Ramakrishna Mission. Its Vedanta philosophy attracted, among many, Gerald Heard, Aldous Huxley, George Harrison, and Christopher Isherwood, in whose summary of Vivekananda's experience at Kanya Kumari one can sense the contrary pulls of the western and eastern ideals mentioned by Tagore, inspired in Vivekananda by the moods of the Indian Ocean around that rock.

India's greatness is fundamentally religious, but religion is not what India needs in her present state of weakness. India needs education, to enable her to help herself. However, this education will be worthless unless it is directed by people who are living in the spirit of Indian religion, as demonstrated by Ramakrishna; people who have trained themselves in the sciences of the West without losing that spirit, people who have renounced all worldly ties and advantages and dedicated themselves utterly to service. Such people must, obviously, be monks, working together within an organisation. Who should provide the funds for this organisation? The nations of the West – because India has something equally valuable to offer them in exchange; the spirit of her religion. The West is dangerously weakened, by a lack of spirituality, just as India is weakened by a lack of food. The nations of the West must be persuaded that, if India collapses, they too will collapse. When once they truly believe this, they will stop trying to exploit India. The exchange of values will begin and the whole world will benefit from it.

The Ramakrishna Mission's monument to Vivekananda's conversion – a very solid and neatly hewn temple housing an eight-foot statue of the beturbaned Swami in bronze and a footprint of Devi, the goddess – is imposing but unsympathetic. Arrows painted on the ground – though the risk of falling in is negligible – manage to suggest an airport runway and the mental rigidity of some of those who have followed Vivekananda, and indeed some of his own less convincing pronouncements. But the setting, with nothing but ocean between you and Africa, Australia or Antarctica, is still magnificent and no doubt awe-inspiring in a monsoon squall.

Gandhi came to Kanya Kumari in January 1937, in the midst of a pilgrimage to Travancore, to rid the state's temples of their bar on Untouchability. His comments are now famous. 'I am writing this at the Cape, in front of the sea, where three waters meet and furnish a sight unequalled in the world. For, this is no port of call for vessels. Like the goddess, the waters around are virgin. The Cape has no population worth the name. The place is eminently fitted for contemplation.' To which Marco Polo's ruder comment might be appended, written over five hundred years before: 'this is not a highly civilised place but decidedly savage'. Its population, he noted, was of fascinating apes called 'Paul cats' and abundant lions, leopards and lynxes.

Gandhi's feeling for the sea, which was also demonstrated by his Salt March in 1930, probably dates from his early years. He was born at the western end of India's coastline, in Porbandar, where a temple has been built with a *sikara* 79 feet high to indicate the age at which he died. In 1869 it was a small princely state in the Kathiawar Peninsula of Gujarat, with a harbour that had been for centuries the springboard for and receptacle of trade with the Middle East and Africa. Its lanes, bazaars, buildings and temples are not very impressive but the soft white stone used in the city's construction has acquired, with the passage of time and the lashing of the Arabian Sea, a rock-like impregnability and the soft hue of pure white marble. It sparkles in sunshine and glows in moonlight; hence Porbandar's name, The White City.

With this maritime background it may seem curious that Gandhi's decision in 1888 to cross the seas to London to study as a barrister was so controversial within his caste. His mother made him swear solemn vows to abstain from wine, women and meat there and then gave her blessing, but his caste tribunal in Bombay outcast him.

Some idea of the unpredictable nature of this Hindu taboo on sea-travel, which underlies Hindu India's relationship to the sea throughout the centuries, can be gained from V.S. Naipaul's masterpiece of life in a traditional Indian immigrant household in Trinidad, *A House for Mr Biswas*. The following incident is set in the late 1940s. The family matriarch Mrs Tulsi, a supposedly orthodox Hindu, has been educating her son for some years in a Roman Catholic college:

> Then came the news that Mrs Tulsi had decided to send Owad abroad to study to become a doctor. And at Arwacas some of Mrs Tulsi's retainers defected. Forgetting that they were in Trinidad, that they had crossed tha black water from India and had thereby lost all caste, they said they could have nothing more to do with a woman who was proposing to send her son across the black water. 'Water off a duck's back,' Mr Biswas said to Shama. 'The number of times that mother of yours has made herself outcast.' There was talk about the suitability and adequacy of the food Owad would get in England. 'Every morning in England, you know,' Mr Biswas said, 'the scavengers go around picking up the corpses. And you know why? The food is not cooked by orthodox Roman Catholic Hindus.'

No doubt similar internal conflicts of self-interest and curiosity with inertia and caution have racked many Indians intending to travel abroad, especially during the more caste-conscious periods of their history. Just as future historians of the British in India will find it hard to generalize about the motives of those who went out there and the extent to which they carried 'little England' with them, so historians of today cannot agree on the extent of Indian taboos against sea-travel, even during a particular period, and, by extension, the influence or otherwise of the Indian Ocean on Indian civilization. In general terms we know there was a decline in Hindu seapower and seafaring up to the coming of the Europeans in the sixteenth century; navigation became more and more the province of the Arabs. But it is quite clear that many Hindu *banias*, the merchant class, and even Brahmins, travelled in ships in the sixteenth and seventeenth centuries, and Hindus frequently financed ships that were captained and crewed by Muslims. Marco Polo's characteristically intriguing glimpse of the Malabar coast around 1300 seems to support this picture: 'Most of the people here abstain from drinking wine. They will not admit as a witness or a guarantor either a wine-drinker or one who sails on the sea. For they say that a man who goes on the sea must be a man in despair.'

Though many earlier references exist in the Hindu scriptures, the earliest reliable instance of Indian navigation seems to be Alexander the Great's return journey to the Euphrates. While he marched overland, his Admiral Nearchus sailed home in a flotilla of boats constructed by native craftsmen of the Punjab.

Nearly four centuries later, in AD 45, a breakthrough in navigation occurred, which was to lead to a huge trade between Rome and the East. This was the discovery, attributed to Hippalus, of the monsoon winds. It is possible that the information had also reached Alexandria through a different route via a stranded Indian sailor.

From around this period the merchants and seamen of Roman Egypt came to know India well, and Indians, including fortune-tellers, conjurors, prostitutes and an ascetic who burnt himself to death in Athens, made the opposite journey to Rome herself, and also settled in Alexandria. A remarkable seaman's guide, compiled at the end of the 1st century by an anonymous Greek author, *The Periplus of the Erythrean Sea,* gives insights into the thriving ports of the Tamil kings of south-east India.

The main trade requirements of the West then, as they continued to be fifteen hundred years later, were spices, perfumes, jewels and fine textiles. Lesser luxuries, such as sugar, rice and ghee were also exported, as well as ivory, both raw and worked. 'In return for her exports India wanted little but gold,' the historian A.L. Basham tells us in *The Wonder that was India,* '... the balance of trade was very unfavourable to the West and resulted in a serious drain of gold from the Roman Empire. This was recognised by Pliny, who, inveighing against the degenerate habits of his day, computed the annual drain to the East as 100 million sesterces, "so dearly do we pay for our luxury and our women".' Hoards of Roman gold coins turn up even today in south India. In Trivandrum they are sold illegally for up to Rs 15,000 to tourists. When Rome fell to Alaric the Goth in 408 he raised his siege in exchange for 3,000 pounds of pepper.

During the same period in which contacts were opening up between the West and India, the kingdoms of the east coast of India began to trade with and eventually establish colonies on the islands of Indonesia, in particular Java and Sumatra. For a millennium or so, until the coming of Islam, these islands would be Hindu and Indian in spirit, a part of Greater India. By the 4th century, Sanskrit was their official language. The wonderful art produced by these civilizations includes the Buddhist *stupa* at Borobodur, one of whose glorious panels depicts an Indian ship under full sail.

A parent Hindu dynasty on the mainland, the Pallavas, built a monument in the seventh century which is among India's most captivating, the ancient seaport of Mahabalipuram. The road from Madras approaches it weaving in and out through dark casuarina plantations and wide green paddy fields, now and then skirting the open sea. Unfortunately, what must originally have been an elegant town is now a scruffy modern village with the caves and sculptures scattered within and around it. The *raths* (temples) which gave the site the name 'the Seven Pagodas' (attributed to mariners by the Daniells who drew it for their famous series of oriental views), seem almost humorous to the untrained eye; they look like cottage loaves or those complicated German cakes with fretted icing. But the most remarkable sculptures are to be found in the great rock-cut panel 'Arjuna's Penance' and, for different reasons, the Shore Temple itself, which is actually on the beach.

'Arjuna's Penance' shows a vast concourse of animals, gods, animal-gods, and sages in motion from both sides towards a central image. It breathes with universal life in the finest traditions of

Indian sculptural naturalism. The story it tells is from the great epic *The Mahabharata*. The heroic Arjuna, after practising extraordinary austerities, comes to beg Siva for the boon of his magic weapon Pinaka so that he may take revenge on the Kauravas. The episode depicted is that in which the birds and animals forget their natural antipathy in the hunter-army marshalled by Siva, Arjuna's divine protector.

The frieze is cut on the vertical faces of two huge boulders, each some 91 feet high and over 152 feet wide. A narrow cleft dividing them from the top to the bottom provides the focal point to which all the figures are hastening. A *nagaraja* and a *nagini* with exceptionally long sinuous tails, the only free-standing sculptures, one above the other in the cleft, seem to be swimming up the waterfall. From the remains of a cistern found on the top of the boulders it seems that on ceremonial occasions water actually did flow.

> At the foot of the cleft, in contrast to the energy and movement of the advancing throngs above, hermitage (*asram*) life flows calmly on beside a stream. A young ascetic fetches water, another wrings out his wet garment, yet another stands, arms raised above his head, staring at the sun, a widespread form of religious self-torture (*tapas*). Others are in the yogic position or with the band called *yogapatta* around their backs and knees, while an aged sage sits in contemplation before a shrine containing a statue of Vishnu – an exceptional case of an image representing an image. (J.C. Harle)

Siva himself is a four-armed figure larger than all the rest, standing slightly to the proper right of the cleft and identified by the long trident over his shoulder and his escort of *ganas*. His left hand is shown making the gift-giving gesture. Before him stands a bearded man on one leg staring at the sun with his arms raised in a semicircle above his head, 'his emaciated body testifying to the rigour of his austerities', as Harle puts it.

The most delightful figures are the animals: tiny baby elephants asleep beneath their mother, a deer delicately scratching its nose with a hind leg, and an emaciated cat on its hind legs with its front paws above its head doing penance like the humans.

The ocean rumbles only a few hundred yards away, and beside it, in fact washed and eroded by it over the centuries (though nowadays not quite directly), is the exquisite Shore Temple with its surrounding wall, on which squat a chain of inscrutable Nandi bulls nose-to-tail; somewhat reminiscent, if they were not so orderly, of the bullocks and cows that wander in every Indian street. The temple itself is in two bits, with a small shrine between them. Though the insides and outsides of the bigger shrines are more lavishly carved, it is the Vishnu image in between, cut out of the bedrock and recumbent on his serpent, that catches the attention. It has a stillness, a primeval power that is somehow magnified by the sound and swell of the sea behind.

This is as it should be. Vishnu it is who creates ambrosia by the Churning of the Ocean in a famous episode in *The Mahabharata*. All the other gods and the demons have been churning for a long time without success. They are tired out and appeal to Brahma to ask Vishnu to give them the necessary burst of strength:

> When they heard the words of Narayana (Vishnu) they became strong, and all together violently stirred the milk of the great ocean once more. Then from the ocean there arose Soma, the calm moon, with its cool rays, and the sun of a hundred thousand rays. And immediately after this the

goddess Sri, dressed in white, appeared from the clarified butter, then the goddess of wine; then Uccaihsravas, the white horse of the sun; and then came the divine shining Kaustubha gem from the chest of the blessed Narayana, blooming with rays, born of the ambrosia. And the great elephant Airavata, with his enormous body and his four white tusks, came forth and was taken by the Wielder of the Thunderbolt.

But as they continued to churn excessively, the terrible Kalakuta poison came forth and immediately enveloped the universe, blazing like a smoky fire; the poison paralysed the triple world with the smell of its fumes. The lord Siva took the form of a sacred chant and held that poison in his throat, and from that time forth he has been known as Blue-throated; thus it is traditionally told. At the request of Brahma and for the sake of protecting all people, Siva swallowed the poison, and from it there arose the Eldest (the goddess of misfortune), her dark form adorned with every kind of gem. (Wendy O'Flaherty)

Such bizarre manifestations emerging out of India would have fitted in quite acceptably with the perception of India of the Arab seafarers who were beginning to make their presence known on the western coast in the seventh century, inaugurating a trade they were to dominate as sailors and merchants until the arrival of the Portuguese in the sixteenth century. They reached Malacca, and China too, at an early stage; there is an Arab reference to the Andaman Islands as early as 871. Freeman-Grenville's translation of an Arab book now known as *The Book of the Wonders of India* allows us to enter this fantastic and dangerous world. Collected in it are a random series of tales – some pithy, some rambling and inconsequential – picked up in the travels of a *nakhoda* or shipmaster of Ramhormuz called Captain Buzurg ibn Shahriyar, probably between 900 and 953. 'It seems,' writes Freeman-Grenville, 'that Buzurg collected sailors' tales much as British sailors collected a rag-bag of miscellaneous odds-and-ends in their ditty boxes.' In fact they share much of the material found in the better-known Sinbad stories. Two of the best tales are redolent of the Arab view of the exotic East. The places mentioned in the tales have not generally been identified with modern sites in India, though Sindabur is known to refer to Goa.

Deadly Snakes

A man from al-Mansura, who had visited Markin, a town several hundred parasangs from the Lar coast where the Ballaha-raya, the King of the Hindus, lives, told me that the mountains there are infested with grey or spotted snakes. If one of these snakes sees a man before the man has seen him, it dies. If the man sees the snake before he has been seen, it is the man who dies. If they see one another at the same moment, they both die. It is the worst of all snakes.

The second tale describes an encounter between an Indian and an Arab sailor that reminds me irresistibly of Professor Godbole, who infuriated Dr Aziz in E. M. Forster's *A Passage to India*:

A lizard prophesies

In India there are many celebrated magicians and sorcerers. I have already said something about them.

Abu Yusuf b. Muslim told me that Abu Bakr al-Fasi had told him at Saymur (Chaul) that Musa al-Sindaburi had related the following to him:

> One day I was talking to the Governor of Sindabur (Goa), when he began to laugh.
> 'Do you know why I was laughing?' he said.
> 'No,' I answered.
> 'Because on the wall there is a lizard, that said: "A foreign guest is going to come."'
> I was surprised by his silliness, and got ready to leave at once. But he said to me:
> 'Do not go until you have seen the end of the matter.'
> We went on talking. One of his people came in and said:
> 'There is a ship in the port just come from Oman.'
> A little later people came in carrying trade goods, materials and rose water. When they opened up the rose water, out came a large lizard that climbed up the wall and joined the first lizard.

The Arab merchants traded with the various coastal emporia of western India, at Cambay, Surat, Goa, Calicut and Cochin among others, and of course further afield. Cambay, in particular, had a role more complex than most other ports, especially after the Moghul conquest of Gujarat in 1572. It became a kind of showpiece for the Moghul emperors who always looked on naval affairs more as a 'pastime' (Nehru's word) that as a serious military and strategic consideration. For instance, Jahangir, the fourth emperor, visited his maritime province of Gujarat to hunt wild elephants and to 'look on the salt sea'. At Cambay his outing was enlivened by a view with which he was not hitherto acquainted: the rising and ebbing of the tides. He also had the experience of sailing on board ship, and visited some Portuguese ships which were in port and had been specially decorated in his honour.

The detail of the Red Sea and East African trade of Cambay given in the *Suma Oriental* brings out its extent and variety, as shown by the economic historian K.N. Chaudhuri. The Cairene merchants brought to Gujarat through Aden such products of Italy, Greece and Syria as gold, silver, mercury, vermilion, copper, rosewater, woollen cloth, glass beads and weapons. Traders from Aden itself dealt in all these commodities, and in addition brought madder, raisins, opium and horses. The return cargo of the Middle Eastern merchants included the economic products of Gujarat and those of the Indonesian archipelago: rice and foodstuffs, cloves, nutmeg, and mace, rare woods, Chinese porcelain, coarse pottery, indigo, carnelian beads and, above all, cotton cloth. The textiles were traded from Aden to Zeila, Berbera, Sokotra, Kilwa, Malindi and Mogadishu and to all places in Arabia.

Muslim pilgrims from India on their way to and from Mecca were also cargo for the Arab vessels. Chaudhuri writes that 'The first personal experience by a landsman of a deep-sea vessel was not always a pleasant one. Abdu'r Razzaq, who made a voyage to India as the Iranian envoy in 1442, "fainted" when he went on board the ship at Hormuz for fear of the sea and the stench of the vessel. The ship carried a cargo of thoroughbred horses [a trade much remarked upon by Marco Polo] and must have been waterproofed, as all ships of the western ocean were, with fish glue and oil.'

Judging from the experience of Tim Severin in 1980, the stench of bilge gas in these traditional Arab *booms* was indeed nauseating. Inspired by the tales of Sinbad, he built a sewn *boom* named

Sohar in Oman out of timber from the Malabar coast with help from the Laccadive Islanders, the only people who still know the technique, and sailed it with an Omani crew 6,000 miles to a rousing welcome in Canton, calling at Calicut *en route*, as a handful of Arab ships still continue to do to load spices, timber and general cargo.

Calicut's merchant community in the 1980s, as Severin says in his most enjoyable account of this adventure, *The Sinbad Voyage*, 'has withered to just two merchant houses – the Baramys and the Koyas. The two families occupy almost identical houses strategically situated on the beach which overlooks the anchorage. Each house is a large low bungalow. Behind it are a courtyard and various sheds in which lie boxes of ship's nails, coils of rope, tins of clarified butter, mysterious packing cases, and a jumble of home-made anchors. The focus of life is the long elegant verandah. Here at all hours of the day, but especially at the time of sunset prayers, can be found a sprinkling of Arab merchants, taking their ease on benches and cane chairs, sipping cups of tea or coffee, and gazing out over the roadstead, where the waves of the Arabian Sea crash and rumble on the beach, and an occasional beggar sidles up to the railings to seek alms in the name of Allah.'

Although the merchants and their dependent trades are so much fewer in Calicut than in the old days, one related custom still survives and prospers; Severin gained considerable inadvertent experience of it. As in the days of Sinbad, Arab sailors can take a wife in every port up to their allotted four, provided they will be properly maintained. All but one of *Sohar*'s Omani crew took advantage of this on arrival in Calicut, borrowing the necessary cash from their captain. No stigma attaches to the fact that the local women may never see their husbands again or at best only very occasionally. Rather, it is socially most acceptable to form an alliance with a family from Arabia. If the husband does not send money from abroad, or better still send for the wife herself, she is free to marry again after three years.

One wonders whether hidden arrangements such as these lay behind the customs that provoked Marco Polo's lively but unlikely account of some aspects of life on the Malabar Coast, which he termed 'the great province of Maabar [*sic*]. You may take it for a fact that it is the richest and most splendid province in the world', which is high praise when you consider that he had probably seen more of the world by then than any man before him. His comment still applies today, though in a more limited sense; thanks to the long-standing and far-sighted policies of the rulers of Travancore, Kerala (modern Malabar) has a literacy rate more than twice the national average and a strong economy based partly on the earnings of Keralites living across the Arabian Sea in the Gulf States.

Cochin, in Kerala, is in fact one of the most restful places I know in India, even on a short visit. The reason seems to be the constant presence of water and, less tangibly, of the past in a half-familiar form. Both are combined if you stay in one of the rooms of the former British Residency (before that the residence of the Dutch Governor from 1744) on Bolghatty Island in the middle of Cochin harbour, which requires you to take a ferry to reach the other parts of the city. This mansion is now pleasantly run-down; and the rooms have windows with leaded glass that seem somehow to let light in from all sides. As the sun sets over the harbour, you can sit comfortably in a garden descending to the water nearby that is lush without being tropical, or slip through beyond the boundary fence to stroll through the other half of the island with lanes of huts and houses alive with people, until you reach the water again: a whole world tucked away from sight. The feeling of water nearby, the drowsy luxuriance of trees and flowers, and the cheerful faces of the Bolghatty Islanders, combine to make the familiar urban press and disorder in this half of the island somehow delightful.

Cochin was the earliest European settlement in India and has been overlaid with first Portuguese, then Dutch, then British influences. It was also one of the first sites of Jewish settlement in India, supposed to have taken place in the sixth century BC , but which certainly dates from the centuries just after the birth of Christ. Today, within the space of a day's travel, one could see a Jewish synagogue, Portuguese churches, Dutch architecture, a couple of mosques, Hindu temples and Chinese fishing nets in the harbour. It would be more appropriate to take a week for such a tour, though; Cochin's pace is definitely not London's or Bombay's – more like that of Madras perhaps.

Its residents must have received quite a shock in the years following its ruler's welcome to the Portuguese, who established their fort there from 1500, some eight centuries or so after the first Arab navigators arrived and began peaceful trading with India. As the impartial Chaudhuri observes: 'The arrival of the Portuguese in the Indian Ocean abruptly ended the system of peaceful oceanic navigation that was such a marked feature of the region.'

The best-known of the Portuguese in India is of course Vasco da Gama, who was the first. He left Lisbon in July 1497 and dropped anchor at Calicut on 18 May 1498 after being piloted across the Indian Ocean from Malindi by an Indian navigator. It is said that two pillars of the old palace in which da Gama was received still remain. On his way there the Portuguese leader knelt down to some Hindu idols, taking them for distorted images of Catholic saints. 'Perhaps they be devils,' said one of his sailors. 'No matter,' said da Gama, 'I kneel before them and worship the true God.'

He died at Cochin in 1524 after nearly a quarter of a century fighting up and down the coast, and was buried at St Francis Church, a building reminiscent of Spanish style, which stands in a quiet spot facing the sea not far from some Chinese fishing nets. His memorial inscription is so plain as to be a little disappointing: 'Here lay buried Vasco da Gama, who died on the Christmas eve of the year AD 1524 at Cochin, until his remains were removed to Portugal fourteen years later.' There is no attempt to dignify him with titles and deeds or to romanticise his roamings, and perhaps that is as it should be because he was, like most of the Portuguese in India (and the British of the time), responsible for some formidable barbarities. After capturing some unarmed ships returning from Mecca, da Gama, in the words of the Portuguese record of the time, 'made the ships empty of goods, prohibited anyone from taking out of them any Moor and then ordered them set fire to.' K. M. Panikkar, an Indian historian of nationalist sentiments, comments: 'In the history of piracy it will be difficult to find a parallel to the barbarism of this Portuguese hero.'

The Portuguese in India are paradoxical, as anyone who considers the successes of the Jesuit Fathers there must agree. As colonists they lasted, strictly speaking, longer than the British Raj; Goa was not finally taken over by the Republic of India until 1961. They also seem to evoke admiration as well as censure in some Indians of a kind different from that directed at the British. That their elite were extreme racists cannot be doubted from the record, that they converted Hindus to Catholicism by some very un-Christian methods is well understood, yet they did, in many cases, marry locally and settle in India from as early as 1509, which few of the British did. When Akbar conquered Gujarat in 1572, about sixty Portuguese were found to have stayed behind in Cambay to look after their affairs. As the journalist Khushwant Singh says, referring to his first and somewhat reluctant   13 visit to Goa (such was its advance write-up as a beauty-spot): 'The Portuguese were vandals. They destroyed more temples and mosques than Ghazni and Ghori put together. They made forcible conversions and slew those who refused to accept Christianity. But, like the Muslim conquerors, they made India their home. They married Indians, brought up their children here and died here. That is why Goa is at once more Indian and Portuguese than the Anglo-Indian metropolises, Calcutta, Bombay, Madras or New Delhi.'

Perhaps – for the subject is by no means settled by historians – the ritual and excess of Catholicism as compared to what Protestantism offered later, touched something in the Indians who encountered it. The very fact that da Gama could confuse a Hindu image with that of a Catholic saint is suggestive. And what else is the regular exposing of the body of the abnormally slow-decaying St Francis Xavier (minus the toe bitten off by an over-enthusiastic devotee but later retrieved) but a quasi-Hindu ritual? V. S. Naipaul's Mrs Tulsi and her son Owad (who wears a crucifix and many other lucky charms) would understand and approve. And in the church of San Francisco d' Assisi in Goa, which began life as a mosque and is now neither a mosque nor a church but a museum, you may see what Manohar Malgonkar describes as 'the figures of Apostles carved in aromatic woods standing cheek-by-jowl with stone images of dancing Sivas and Ganesh, the elephant god.'

Only the churches now remain to give one some inkling of Goa in its heyday, when the tolling of the bells indicated that the Inquisitors were about to perform yet another *auto-da-fé*; though surprisingly, the full rigour of the Inquisition was felt only by baptised subjects of the Portuguese Empire. Goa in the late sixteenth century became *Ilha Illustrissima*, *Senhora de code o Oriento*, the Rome of the East and *Dourada*, the City of Gold. 'All the races of the world are here,' wrote Linschoten, the Dutch traveller who visited Goa in 1583. 'There is a great fair every day, a kind of *bourse*, where men from all parts of the world make their market. The tongues are babel and the noise deafening. *Hidalgos* swagger [no Englishman would do that] on horseback and even their horse-cloths are trimmed with pearls. Ladies float *en boddice*, on ornamented open palanquins.'

Goa survived the excesses of the Inquisition and the loss of Portuguese supremacy in India, as well as the excesses of the *hidalgos*, the Portuguese nobility, and subsided into a languid decay which was memorably, if melodramatically, captured in the film *Trikal* by the Bombay-based film-director Shyam Benegal. In it a high-born Goan family who are virtually oblivious to the rumoured Indian takeover, still insist, after centuries of living in Goa, that their son should marry a bride from the mother-country – with dire results. Post-takeover, in reality the city flourished as a smuggler's port servicing an entire subcontinent living in Gandhian austerity with western luxuries, as India had done for Rome nearly two thousand years before.

Bassein, the even more splendid *Corte de Norte* – the Chief City of the North – settled by the Portuguese in 1534 on the coast immediately to the north of Bombay, was not as fortunate as Goa. Today it is a massive and desolate overgrown ruin of arches, gateways, churches and gravestones: Portuguese baroque run riot in the jungle. Heber, Bishop of Calcutta, who visited Bassein in the 1820s, is reported by Stella Snead to have written: 'they are melancholy objects to look at, but they are monuments nevertheless of departed greatness, of a love of splendour far superior to the anxiety for amassing money by which other nations have been chiefly actuated, and of a zeal for God...' A bold judgment no doubt coloured by the East India Company's rapacity in Bengal not long before, but not entirely accurate. Bassein, unlike Goa, was a city where none but Christians were permitted to live. Most of its inhabitants were blue-blooded *hidalgos*, and it seems that their religious intolerance and corruption, not their saintliness, destroyed them when the city fell bloodily to the Marathas in 1739.

Before coming to Madras and Bombay, the two ports which the British created about a century after the founding of Bassein, and which are both prospering today in their different ways, it is worth remembering that there was also a spate of Hindu building at this time. The glorious pillared corridors of the great temple at Rameshwaram on an island in the Palk Strait date from the seventeenth century. Temple-building continued much later in the south of India than the north, where the Muslim invasions put a stop to it from about the fourteenth century. The superbly carved corridors of Rameshwaram, nearly 4,000 feet in length, are the work of the Nayaka dynasty of Madurai. They surround a temple, begun by a prince of Ceylon and completed in 350 years, the focus of which is the *lingam*, said to have been installed by Rama himself. From Rameshwaram he crossed the 'fathomless' ocean to Lanka on a bridge, built of trees and rocks by his monkey followers, which now forms Adam's Bridge. On his way back, after killing the demon-king Ravana and rescuing his wife Sita, he is supposed to have stopped at Rameshwaram to worship Siva and expiate his sin. Today the place is so holy that every particle of sand on the island is regarded as part of the *Sivalingam*. Rameshwaram is almost as great a magnet for devout Hindus as Benares is.

Bombay, like the temple at Rameshwaram, is built on an island, in fact originally seven islands, and is a magnet of a different sort. Eight million people are now crammed into it or bursting out of it: many of them lured from rural poverty by the prospect of a better life. It is India's richest and fastest-moving city, a real contemporary City of Gold, to recall both the Portuguese name for Goa at its zenith and that of Gillian Tindall's illuminating and richly detailed biography of Bombay. With its Victorian edifices and its skyscrapers, is it essentially a western city like London or New York with Indian additions, or an Indian city dressed in western externals? Tindall settles for the latter, concluding her book with the comment of the editor of the Westminster Gazette who visited Bombay with the press party for the 1911 Durbar of George V:

> In spite of alien rule, Bombay strikes you as eminently belonging to itself, as being in fact a real Indian town; and as remote as possible from a British colony. This, perhaps, is the greatest tribute that can be paid to the English who made it, or at least made it possible.

To put it another, Indian way – that of Khushwant Singh – which chimes perfectly with my own sensations as a relative newcomer sniffing the warm, pungent ocean breeze from Back Bay at sunrise from a high-rise luxury flat in *filmi* Malabar Hill:

> Each time I return home and drive through the stench of bare-bottomed defecators that line the road from Santa Cruz airport to the city I ask myself:
>
>> *Breathes there a man with a soul so dead*
>> *Who never to himself hath said*
>> *This is my own, my native land?*
>
> I can scarcely breathe, but I yell, 'Yeah, this is my native land. I don't like it, but I love it!'

Though the British built it (mainly on a base of rotten fish and the leaves of the coconut palm), the Portuguese founded it. Their first contact, in 1509, set the tone of much that followed. Vasco da Gama made a 'rapacious foray' (as Tindall describes it) in which, to quote da Gama, 'our men captured many cows and some blacks who were hiding among the bushes, and of whom the good were kept and the rest were killed.' The Portuguese owned it until 1662, when it formed part of the dowry brought by the Portuguese princess Catherine of Braganza to Charles II. Her countrymen in India were reluctant to part with it and cherished hopes of buying it back. But 'the Honourable John Company' – a phrase deriving from Sir John Child, the Governor of Bombay, who died there in 1690 – soon scotched these hopes by leasing it themselves from the British Crown for £10 annually and administering it from their factory at Surat.

According to Tindall it was the Company's monopoly on trade with India that prevented Bombay from acquiring its due importance earlier than it did in the mid-nineteenth century. Even in 1825 it was described in the Directory as being 'of little importance to the Company'. With the fading away of 'the last wraith' of the Company in 1858 'like the grin of the Cheshire Cat', in Tindall's evocative phrases, and with the coming of steamers and the opening of the Suez Canal in 1869, Bombay's phenomenal growth became assured.

This was the kind of city in which Rudyard Kipling was born in 1865 and which he looked back to all his life with nostalgia:

> Surely in toil or fray
> Under an alien sky,
> Comfort it is to say:
> 'Of no mean city am I!'
> Neither by service nor fee
> Come I to mine estate –
> Mother of cities to me
> For I was born in her gate,
> Between the palms and the sea,
> Where the world-end steamers wait.

By that time Bombay had long been both a port and a city of shipbuilding. Bombay frigates built by the famous Parsi Wadia family, who came to Bombay from Gujarat (and originally from Persia around AD 650), fought at the battle of Trafalgar. Tindall writes of one that 'sailed the world for years with the following secret message carved on her kelson by the chief shipwright: "The ship was built by a d---d Black Fellow AD 1800".'

The debate that has been a continuous refrain in Bombay's history concerns its chronic lack of space and, in particular, the political and technical feasibility of reclaiming land from the sea, a process begun from 1662 with the gradual fusion of the seven islands. In the 1940s reclamation created the elegant Marine Drive along part of the sweep of Back Bay; unfortunately, it peters out in an unfinished sea wall. Most recently, in Colaba, a cluster of skyscrapers at Nariman Point has been thrown up on land taken from the sea. The famous view of the city on arrival by sea constantly changes with new buildings, though their impact on Bombay's urban crush seems minimal. Tindall's verdict on the land-from-the-sea so far is harsh and probably quite just: 'it has had no effect on the rest of Bombay, nor was it ever likely to: its rationale is not sensible use of valuable land but municipal, federal or national hubris.'

16

Madras, by contrast, seems closer to the nineteenth century than to the twentieth; in many ways it is still a colonial city of the British Raj, unaware of the wider world. One of its best-known inhabitants, because of his regular newspaper column, and the city's only resident Englishman, Harry Miller (who settled there post-Raj with an Indian wife after service in the British merchant-navy), once told me of his attempt to adjust the rules of the Madras Club to accept Indian national dress for dinner. The rest of the club committee, Indian to a man, preferred to maintain suits and ties. One of my own cherished memories of Madras is of overhearing a beefy-looking (though I am sure he didn't touch the stuff) police inspector in a darkened hotel restaurant at lunchtime stubbornly resisting the pleas of an Indian-born consultant sent from London for a licence for a live band to play pop-music. The policeman apparently feared the effect on Madrasis of what he termed 'erotic rhythms'.

There are times, in fact, when one could be forgiven for thinking that there has been relatively little disturbance in the city since the days of Robert Clive, who twice tried to shoot himself in the Writers Building to escape debt, and eventually married in St Mary's Church in Fort St George. It seems appropriate that the insular, detached and charming novelist R.K. Narayan, who was 80 in 1987, should have spent much of his childhood in Madras. As he wryly observes of his fellow-Madrasis during the First World War, they 'did not really realise that the city was being shelled from the sea' by the German warship *Emden*. 'Their urge to flee the city was in keeping with an earlier move, when the sea was rough with cyclone and it was prophesied that the world would end that day, and many had their carriages harnessed and all valuables packed in readiness to drive off to Conjeevaram, forty miles away, the moment the sea should be noticed to rise and advance towards the city.'

Maritime colonial life under the Raj outside the cities was a lot less decorous, both for the rulers and for the ruled. No more vivid guide to this can be found than the *Memoirs of a Bengal Civilian*. John Beames, its angular author, was appointed Collector at Balasore in 1869 on the coast of Orissa a few hundred miles south of Calcutta. Salt was made there on the seashore under strict licence, as it is all round the Indian coastline in varying quantities. It was a lonely job.

> The salt-lands are like a picture in *The Illustrated London News* I remember many years ago of 'Bulgarian fishermen on the lower Danube' … Huge, sluggish stream – 'boom of the bittern' generally – dark evening – streak of light on the horizon, and that sort of thing. The salt-lands are wild, grassy plains; sandhills by the seashore; foul creeks half salt, half fresh; alligators – black, shiny mud – melancholy great sea, roaring and tumbling far off across wet sands – somehow it seems always to be low water. In the opposite direction is the one redeeming feature, a beautiful little range – far off – of the bluest of blue hills behind which the sun is just setting.

Beames's melancholy duty as a local magistrate was to convict poverty-stricken shore-dwellers of making small quantities of salt for themselves illegally – the very act which Mahatma Gandhi repeated by the sea in Gujarat as a symbol of British exploitation, with such intuitive understanding of its power to unite Indians. Beames objected to these 'petty acts of oppression' and, after a 'lengthy correspondence' with the Board of Revenue, put a stop to them.

A few years later he was posted not far away, inland to Cuttack, where he found himself in overall charge of the coast at False Point, a long sandy spit at the mouth of the Mahanadi River, so-named because ships used to confuse it for Point Palmyras, fifty miles to the north, and become wrecked.

Its real authority was not so much Beames at Cuttack as a Captain Harris on the spot, an old skipper who had sailed the Indian Ocean from Suez and the Cape to Hong Kong and Batavia.

Beames's introduction to Captain Harris was characteristic of both of them and of 'up–country' existence in the *mofussil* away from Calcutta:

> It was on the occasion of my going to False Point with Ravenshaw when he went on leave. Our steamer arrived there at dusk, and anchored in the great dreary lagoon. Not very far off was the flat *Ghazipore*, and on the deck under an awning sat a man at a table silhouetted against the dim light of a ship's lantern hung over his head. On the table was a water bottle and glass and under the table a small keg. With the regularity of a mechanical toy, the man stooped and turned the tap of the keg so that liquor ran into his glass, then filled up the glass with water and drank it. After a short rest, during which he smoked a pipe, he repeated the process. We had just finished our dinner on the steamer, and as we smoked our cheroots we all sat on deck and watched with much amusement this solitary figure on the flat. Presently, out of the darkness a boat approached us, and a message was handed up to the effect that Captain Harris would like to see Mr Faulkner if he was on board. So old Faulkner went off in the boat. After a short time we saw him emerge from the darkness on to the deck of the flat where he took a chair opposite the solitary figure, and then *two* glasses were regularly filled at the keg and regularly emptied. Perhaps they heard the roar of laughter from the steamer with which we greeted this new development, for a curtain was suddenly let down which hid them from our sight.

To the north-east of False Point lie the many mouths of the Ganges and, upriver, after exceedingly tricky navigation of the Hooghly (as the Ganges is known near its end), Calcutta, the destination of all the ships looked after by Captain Harris. The point at which Mother Ganga is considered finally to merge with the Ocean is at the southernmost tip of Sagar Island, known as Ganga Sagar, 85 miles directly south of Calcutta. The inevitable temple stands there, and a bathing festival takes place annually. So did child sacrifice until the nineteenth century; it was officially outlawed by Lord Bentinck in 1829 along with the more notorious *suttee*. The island and the temple have not had a peaceful history. A devastating flood in 1688 killed almost the entire population. Rehabilitation started in 1811, when much of the jungle (which is still the haunt of the famous man-eating Royal Bengal Tiger) was cleared and the present road to the temple built. But in 1864 it was again overwhelmed by a terrible cyclone when only 1,500 out of the 5,600 inhabitants survived.

Rabindranath Tagore knew and loved the place, the southern extremity of the riverine water-scape of East Bengal that inspired his most lyrical poems and letters as he floated about his family estates. One of these letters, written in October 1891, beautifully encapsulates the bond between men and water in Indian life:

> When I come to the country I cease to view man as separate from the rest. As the river runs through many a clime, so does the stream of men babble on, winding through woods and villages and towns. It is not a true contrast that 'men may come and men may go, but I go on for ever'. Humanity, with all its confluent streams, big and small, flows on and on, just as does the river, from its source in birth to its sea of death; – two dark mysteries at either end, and between them various play and work and chatter unceasing.

ANDREW ROBINSON

BOOKS QUOTED

Arranged below in the order first quoted in the text:

Creative Unity by Rabindranath Tagore (London, 1922)
The Ochre Robe by Aghenanda Bharati (London, 1961)
Ramakrishna and His Disciples by Christopher Isherwood (London, 1965)
Marco Polo – The Travels trans. by R. E. Latham (London, 1958)
A House for Mr Biswas by V. S. Naipaul (London, 1961)
The Wonder that was India by A. L. Basham (London, 3rd Edn, 1967)
The Art and Architecture of the Indian Subcontinent by J. C. Harle (London, 1986)
Hindu Myths trans. by Wendy O'Flaherty (London, 1975)
The Book of the Wonders of India trans. by G. S. P. Freeman-Grenville (London, 1981)
Trade and Civilisation in the Indian Ocean by K. N. Chaudhuri (Cambridge, 1985)
The Sinbad Voyage by Tim Severin (London, 1982)
India and the Indian Ocean by K. M. Panikkar (London, 1945)
Editor's Page by Khushwant Singh (Bombay, 1981)
Dead and Living Cities by Manohar Malgonkar (Delhi, 1977)
Ruins in Jungles by Stella Snead (London, 1962)
City of Gold by Gillian Tindall (London, 1982)
My Days by R. K. Narayan (London, 1975)
The Memoirs of a Bengal Civilian by John Beames (London, Pbk Edn, 1984)
Glimpses of Bengal by Rabindranath Tagore (London, 1921)

The Blue Immanence

by Ashvin Mehta

The sea I have loved since my childhood, and photographed mostly in black-and-white since the early 1960s, is the sea of abstract designs on changing areas of wet sand formed by ebbing waters at low tide, of criss-crossing streamlets or eddies around rocks, of patterns formed on the beach by wind and grass, insects and pebbles. It is the silent, primeval sea, stark, beautiful and unchanged over the ages, belonging to no land and no time, and totally devoid of any human element. When the present book was proposed, I was hesitant. I wanted the presence of the 'other', the public sea to grow upon me, before I started my work. I wanted my inner vision to adjust to new parameters of colour, distance and the human presence. This happened after nearly ten months of waiting, and I agreed to photograph the coast of India, along its 6000 km.-long sandy, rocky and marshy stretch of land and on islands nearby.

Among my encounters with seething humanity were those at Ganga Sagar during the annual fair on Makar Sankranti (14 January); at Puri, where thousands daily greet the rising sun with folded hands; at Chowpatti, Bombay, when idols of Ganesh are immersed in the sea; and at Dwarka on 'Gokul Ashtami', the day Lord Krishna was born. I could experience how the sea itself became, for the devotee, the vast body of the deity he worshipped; bathing in the sea was a way of touching and communicating with it. At these and many other places of pilgrimage, associated with both Hindu and non-Hindu shrines – such as Velankani (Christian) and Nagore (Muslim) in Tamilnadu – it was difficult not to be swept away by the religious fervour of pilgrims.

Among fishing communities all over the country – whether out of gratitude or out of fear of the elements, or both – reverence for the sea, as a concrete form of the formless Reality, is most prevalent. It cuts across all barriers of religion and expresses itself in a number of customs and rituals and festivals. In particular I was struck by the aesthetic expression of this reverence by the fishermen of Bengal (plate 70), who carve the hull of their ships in the form of a goddess, and dress it with clothes and flowers. I came to love the fishermen of Gopalpur and Chorwad, of Goa and Karwar, and my initial reaction to their bare weather-bitten bodies and the pervading stench of fish, gave way to silent admiration for their way of life. I felt that they may be reflecting the wisdom of a Shankaracharya or a Krishnamurti – that the insecure are truly free, that every day is a new day with joys and challenges all its own. At times, without any forethought, I joined family members in anxiously awaiting the fishermen's return from a catch, or became excited when they obtained a good price at the fish auction!

Among the most memorable images I cherish as a photographer, and the places I long to visit again as an individual are Calangute, Goa (plate 23), during the summer months; Rameshwaram (plate 49) around Pongal festival; Ganga Sagar (plate 69), during the annual winter fair, and Puri (plate 61) during the Puja holidays. Here, as nowhere else, have I felt the bonds of the land of my birth the strongest. I experienced as though I was never born and will never die. Time flowed through me, leaving me untouched.

During the course of eight months I worked on this book, there were many moments of ecstatic joy. For hours I was all alone, a silent witness to the great order manifesting itself in the tides of the sea, in the life-cycles of its insects and plants, and in the seasonal changes. It was then that the vast sheet of water before me was transformed into the blue immanence, and submerged me totally. The images I offer are but a pale reflection of this sparkling and invigorating experience.

19

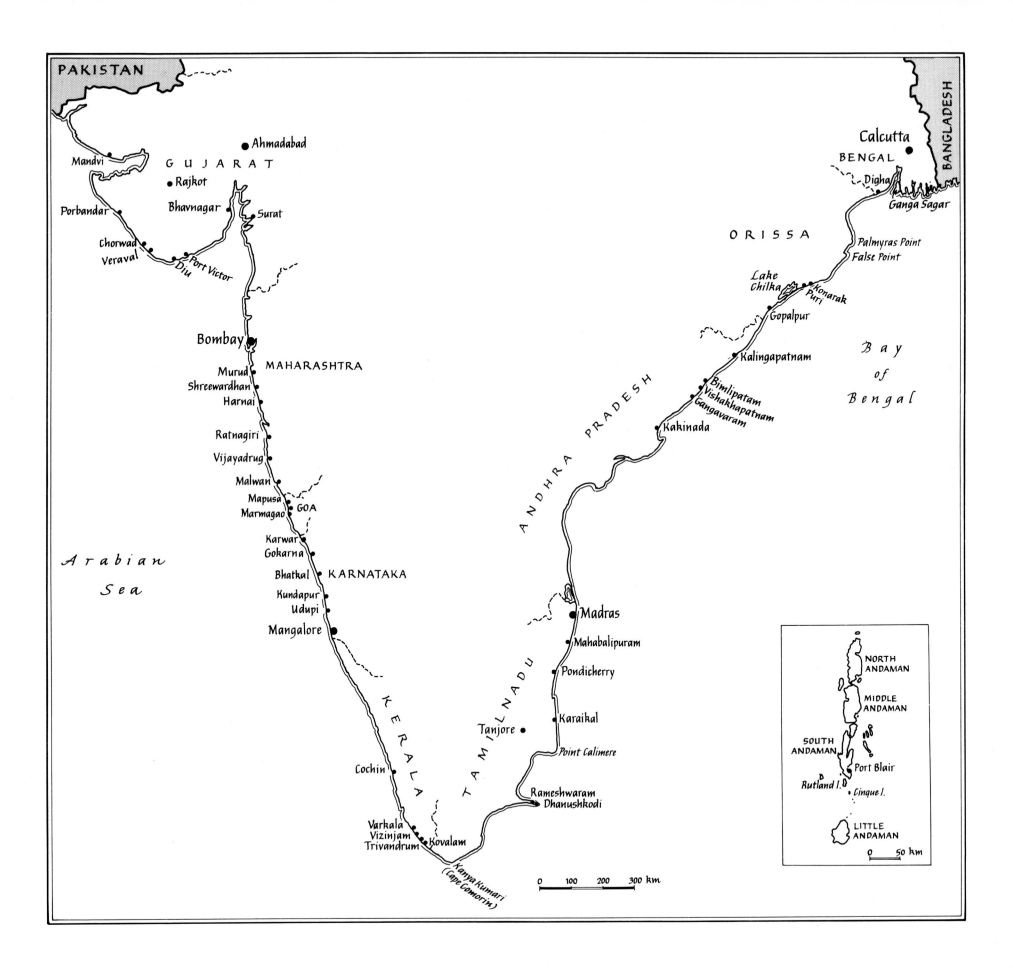

Captions

Gujarat (Plates 1 to 10)

1. Chorwad, on the Saurashtra coast of Gujarat, is known mainly for giant waves breaking against algae-covered rocks. It has a small community of fishermen and an old palace, now converted into a hotel.
2. The entire coastal region of Saurashtra is rich in limestone, the basic raw material for cement and soda ash. This quarry near Porbandar, with quaintly sculpted forms, is so close to the sea that one can hear the roaring waters during high tide.
3. On the eighth day of Chaitra (in April), a fair takes ·place at Kanek, Chorwad. The women resting in the shade are from the Ghediya Koli community, who usually grow and sell betel-leaf, or 'pan', one of the main cash-crops of the region.
4. This colourful deity of Kankeshwari in Diu, an ex-Portuguese settlement, is in a sea-cut grotto. Twice a day the waters at high tide enter the cave and almost wash the deity's feet. This natural 'temple' becomes inaccessible when the south-west monsoon lashes the coast.
5. The beach at Jhanjmer, near Bhavnagar, has a rocky ridge running parallel to the sea, where wind and sea and rains have together carved beautiful honeycomb crevices. Parrots, swifts and swallows nestle there during the dry months of the year.
6. At Alang, near Bhavnagar, is located one of the two shipbreaking yards in India. It is comparable to any major yard in the world, and at least twenty-five to thirty big ships are being torn down there at any given time.
7. The open-air shrine of Nakalank, near Ghogha, Bhavnagar, is about a kilometre from the coast on a rocky shelf, which becomes submerged during high tide. During low tide, as at Digha, West Bengal, the waters recede a few kilometres from the shore and one can walk down to this shrine of Lord Siva.
8. Rupali of Chanch, near Port Victor, has green eyes and is true to her name, which means 'beautiful girl'.
9. A unique shepherd colony on the seacoast of Kutch, at Tundavandh near Mandvi. The houses, known as Bhunga, are made of mud and animal droppings, and are very comfortable even in extremes of temperature (as low as 0°C during the winter and as high as 48°-50°C in the summer). Sheep and goats thrive on grass and shrubs that grow along the barren, salty coastline.
10. Flamingos visit many coastal towns of Saurashtra during the winter, and young ones remain even in the summer under the supervision of a few matron-birds. This flock of around 2,000 or more at Porbandar live on algae which grow in effluents from the soda ash factory. Unlike the migratory visitors at Point Calimere Sanctuary (plate 51), these flamingos are not at all frightened by the human presence.

Maharashtra (plates 11 to 18)

11. Ratnagiri, a minor port on the coast of Maharashtra, is best known as the birthplace of Lokmanya Tilak, one of the early leaders of the Indian Congress. This view of the new jetty is taken from the Bhagwati Fort.
12. The champak tree *(Plumeria acutifolia)* at Harihareshwar, near Shreewardhan. Harihareshwar is an important place of pilgrimage on the Maharashtra coastline, and has a hillock jutting out in the sea, which was neatly cut into two by some prehistoric upheaval.
13. Immersion of Lord Ganesh in the Back Bay at Chowpatti, Bombay, with skyscrapers in the background. On the fourteenth day of Bhadrapad (August–September), thousands of idols are carried in an unending procession and immersed in the sea.
14. Maharashtra has some of the best sea-forts of India; this one at Vijayadrug was constructed by Sivaji, the seventeenth-century Maratha chief.
15. The open-air fishing market at Harnai, north of Ratnagiri, is the most unusual one on the entire coastline of India. At many other fishing centres fish is sold on the sandy beaches, but nowhere else are they sold right in the middle of the bay.
16. The sea-fort of Sindhudurg, built on a rocky island off Malwan, near Ratnagiri, was a formidable naval base of Sivaji, who personally selected the site and participated in its construction.
17. Colourful rocks off Malwan, near Sindhudurg, some covered with lime-green algae.
18. The sea-fort of Janjira, near Murud, was built by the Nawab of Janjira in the late seventeenth century. It was considered impregnable in those days.

Goa (plates 19 to 26)

19. Bogmalo, near the airport, is one of Goa's more attractive and less frequented beaches.
20. Marmagao port handles all the export of iron ore from the mines of Goa.

21

21. Thousands of seagulls flock near the jetty at Betul, where fishermen land with their catch.
22. View to the north from the Chapora Fort, near Mapusa. Cashew trees in the foreground flourish in Goa's undulating hilly terrain.
23. Villagers from the hinterland crowd the beaches of Goa before the onset of the monsoon. It is a social custom, and not a religious ritual, to bathe and bury oneself in warm sand alternately a few times a day on at least four weekends in the months of April and May. This group at Calangute spent the whole day cooking, eating and resting on the beach itself.
24. Returning home with a catch at Colva. Goa has a rich culinary tradition of sea foods.
25. Vagator beach, at the foot of the Chapora Fort, has some unusually coloured rocks. Potable water collects in shallow pools in the early morning.
26. This old lighthouse in the Aguada Fort is located on a hill near the mouth of the Mandovi River, and is architecturally unique among the many lighthouses that dot the Indian coastline.

Karnataka (plates 27 to 34)

27. Columnar lava at Coconut Island, off Malpe, near Udupi, is a national geological monument. The rock that constitutes the columns was formed 60 million years ago as a result of volcanic activity.
28. Bhatkal Beach, as seen from a hillock with black basaltic rocks and 'madar' flowers (*Calotropis prosera*) in the foreground. In ancient times, Bhatkal was a major sea-trading centre on the western coast.
29. Fishermen loading a truck with their catch at Malpe, near Udupi. The sea-areas surrounding Malpe are the richest fisheries in India, and Malpe is the largest fish-curing port in the country.
30. Though not well-known, Gujjadi, near Kundapur, has one of the most scenic beaches in Karnataka. In comparison, the nearby beach of Marvanthe, though popular, is monotonously straight and without any character.
31. There are many well-sheltered bays south of Karwar, and a new naval base is being built here. This rocky promontory is near Gokarna.
32. At Gangulli, near Kundapur. Before the onset of monsoon, the drying, grading and storing of sardines is at its peak. The women workers use the outer cover of coconut blossoms as headwear to protect them from the scorching sun.

33. The Kali River meeting the sea at Sadashivgad, Karwar. Rabindranath Tagore wrote his first drama in 1883 in the wooded surroundings of Karwar, which has a fine all-weather harbour.
34. Tribal women of the Halaki Gowda community at Gokarna during the annual Mahasivratri festival. Gokarna, considered the Varanasi (Benares) of south India, is an important Siva pilgrimage centre.

Kerala (plates 35 to 40)

35. Chinese fishing nets around the harbour of Cochin. They were introduced by traders from the court of Kublai Khan. At night, a light attached to the central rod serves to attract fish into the net.
36. Aerial view of the typical Kerala coastline, south of Kovalam, Trivandrum, with backwaters, coconut groves and the Western Ghats in the background.
37. A mixed plantation of banana and coconut trees with young banana plants in the foreground. Except for the northern coast of Gujarat, coconut and banana grow in abundance along the entire coastline of India. Banana plants promote the growth of coconut trees by releasing moisture into the atmosphere.
38. At Vizinjam, near Trivandrum. The fishermen of Kerala use huge fishing nets, which they haul at two ends standing on the shore, enclosing the fish in the centre. When the net nears the shore, young boys jump and shout and thump the waters to shock the fish and prevent them from escaping.
39. Varkala, associated with Narayana Guru, a great saint and social reformer, has a beautiful beach with red sandstone cliffs along the shore. In the distance can be seen a typical Kerala fishing net being hauled.
40. Cochin is one of the finest natural harbours in the world, from which the produce of Kerala – spices, coir, rubber and seafood – is exported all over the world.

Tamilnadu, including Pondicherry (plates 41 to 51)

41. A shop selling shells, cowries, corals and souvenirs at Rameshwaram, one of the four major centres of Hindu pilgrimage. There is a coral reef near Rameshwaram, which is an island in the Palk Strait sanctified by Lord Rama after his war against Ravana.
42. Fishing catamarans near Kanya Kumari (or Cape Comorin), the southern tip of the Indian peninsula. At various places on the eastern coast, even two-log

catamarans are used. Sailing on these boats is an intricate exercise in balancing which combines both surf-riding and yachting.
43. Salt-pans north of Kanya Kumari. All the coastal states of India have a thriving salt industry. Sea-water is diverted during high tide, or pumped from creeks, and evaporated by solar heat in open pans scooped out of earthen embankments. The main season for this activity is from December to June on the west coast; on the east, because of the second monsoon, the season is somewhat shorter.
44. The Shore Temple at Mahabalipuram, near Madras, contains two rock-cut shrines – one dedicated to the Lord Siva and the other to Lord Vishnu. Pallava kings built the port of Mahabalipuram in the seventh century, together with other monuments hewn out of solid rock.
45. Karaikal, the former French pocket in Tamilnadu, lies 163 km. south of Pondicherry, and is an ancient pilgrimage centre. The row of palm-tree trunks, buried upside down, prevents erosion of the coastline, and act as a sort of guide for homecoming ships. The boats are also anchored to the trunks.
46. Shreenivas Perumal (Lord Vishnu) during Masimagham festival at Pondicherry, the former French colony. On the full-moon day of Magha (February-March), idols from 38 temples in Pondicherry and surrounding villages are brought to the sea, their feet washed with sea-water and installed, facing east, for a day on the beach. The festival is probably unique in the entire country, because the devotees lend the best of their ornaments to the deities, which are immaculately dressed and decorated with flowers and jewels.
47. The fifteenth-century Ramanathswamy temple at Rameshwaram is famous for its magnificent seventeenth-century corridors, the largest in India: 132 m. north to south and 198 m. east to west. The pillars are remarkable for their elaborate carvings and the ceiling for its colourful geometrical designs, which may have Tantric significance.
48. Vivekananda rock memorial at Kanya Kumari, where the waters of the Arabian Sea (west), the Indian Ocean (south) and the Bay of Bengal (east) meet. It was on one of these rocks that Swami Vivekananda, the apostle of resurgent India, sat in deep meditation in the winter of 1892/93.
49. Performing *sraddha* (a memorial ceremony for dead relatives) at Agnitirtha, on the shore at

Rameshwaram. *Sraddha* performed here has special significance, as it does at Gaya in Bihar.

50. The sand-flats of Dhanushkodi at the southern tip of the island of Rameshwaram, the point where Sri Lanka is closest to India. The *Spinifex* grass, which helps to hold the sand dunes and arrest their movement, is also found on the coast of Kutch in Gujarat. In the Tamil language *Spinifex* is aptly known as 'Ravana's whiskers'!

51. Flamingos, lesser flamingos (more red in colour and smaller in size), spoonbills and Caspian terns at Point Calimere, the only bird sanctuary located right on the seashore. It is 135 km. from Tanjore and has many local birds besides the migratory visitors.

Andhra Pradesh (plates 52 to 57)

52. Fishermen returning after fishing at night to Vishakhapatnam, the port of Andhra Pradesh, which has grown into an industrial metropolis in recent years.

53. Dutch cemetery at Bimlipatam, a seventeenth-century Dutch settlement 24 km. from Vishakhapatnam. In the nineteenth century all the Dutch properties were handed over to the British East India Company.

54. The main characteristic of the coast of Andhra Pradesh is the meandering mountains running close to the sea. Gangavaram, near the Andhra Steel Project, is typical.

55. Coastal Andhra Pradesh has the most beautiful palm groves in the entire country. This one close to the scenic road from Vishakhapatnam to Bimlipatam has grown naturally, like the others, throughout the state.

56. The fishing village of Appikonda, near Kakinada. The external resemblance of individual houses and their placement in relation to one another, compared with those of Kutch in Gujarat (plate 9) is remarkable. Perhaps this architectural style is best suited to give protection against cyclones which frequently ravage the coast of Andhra Pradesh.

57. Drying chillies (red peppers) at Kalingapatnam. Andhra Pradesh chillies are very hot and are freely used in all the local preparations.

Orissa (plates 58 to 68)

58. Lake Chilka, from Barkul. Nestling in the heart of coastal Orissa, Chilka is the largest inland lake in the country. This 1100 sq. km. expanse of brackish water is a vast lagoon, with access to the Bay of Bengal through a narrow mouth. Encircled by picturesque hills, its colour changes with the passing clouds and with the movement of the sun.

59. With the bounteous gifts of mackerel, prawn and crab, Chilka provides a living for thousands of fishermen along its coast. The boats have a rectangular sail of woven mat, unique to Chilka.

60. Fishermen mending their nets under the shade of triangular sails, a scene typical of Orissa, at Gopalpur, easily the most beautiful sea-resort on the eastern coast. During the British Raj it came to be known as Gopalpur-on-Sea.

61. Pilgrims at Puri, one of the four most holy places of India. Like Hardwar on the River Ganga in the north, Puri attracts pilgrims all the year round. They visit the temple of Jagannath, only after a dip in the sea.

62–3. A catch of fish at Konarak, which, though best known for its Sun Temple, is also a major fishing centre on the east coast. Over the centuries, the sea has moved so far away from the Temple that it is difficult to imagine that 700 years ago it stood directly on the sea.

64. A lone fisherwoman at Gopalpur waiting for her husband to return from the sea.

65. The ruins of a mansion, at Gopalpur. In both Gopalpur and Puri, there are imposing ruins ravaged by the sea.

66. Fishermen of Orissa wear conical (and somewhat comical) hats, which distinguish them from those of neighbouring Bengal and Andhra Pradesh. Here they are auctioning their catch at Gopalpur.

67. White marker-poles planted on high sand dunes are used along the coast to guide the homecoming fishermen during daytime. At night, they are guided by the lighthouse at Gopalpur.

68. A village of itinerant fishermen near Konarak in the late evening light of winter. They stay here only during the dry months.

West Bengal (plates 69 to 72)

69. More than 500,000 people, mostly from Uttar Pradesh, Bihar, Bengal and Orissa, gather for a holy dip every year on Makar Sankranti (January 14) at Ganga Sagar, where the River Ganga meets the sea. Ganga Sagar is an island in one of the many mouths of the river, which throws up a new island every few years.

70. Fishermen of Bengal carve the hulls of their ships in the form of a goddess and dress the image with a piece of coloured cloth like a petticoat, and tie on auspicious sheaves of unhusked rice. Most of the names of the boats also end with a suffix meaning 'mother'; rightly so, because it is the boats that sustain the fishermen.

71. Sunset at Digha, the most popular beach resort of Bengal. One can drive 6 km. along this flat, hard beach during low tide without any fear of getting stuck in the sand.

72. Ice-blocks being carried on cycle-rickshaws to the fishing village at Digha, which supplies fish to Calcutta, 240 km. away, in containers filled with crushed ice sprinkled with salt.

Andaman (plate 73 to 80)

73. Teepauk trees, Andaman. The islands of Andaman abound in evergreen forests, some trees reaching the height of 50 m. or more. These trees have large buttresses and stout spreading branches forming a canopy.

74. The Andaman and Nicobar group of 293 islands is near to the equator and spreads over 700 km. north to south. The Twin Islands are located two to three hours by boat from Wandoor, which is an hour's drive from the capital town of Port Blair.

75. Andaman has some of the best preserved mangroves in the world, because of the total absence of pollution. Mangroves anchor the mud in tropical creeks and estuaries. Those near the sea have conical air-absorbing roots that grow vertically upwards.

76. Cinque is one of the most beautiful coral islands of South Andaman.

77. A view of mussel-encrusted rocks from Red Skin Island, one of the many uninhabited islands of South Andaman.

78. A wind-swept forest on Rutland Island, South Andaman. The forest is so dense that sunlight can hardly penetrate to the forest floor.

79. Driftwood at Wandoor, situated on the west coast of the main island of South Andaman. Wandoor beach is full of giant driftwood, which has been thrown up from the nearby forest by the onslaught of wind and rain during monsoon. Andaman, incidentally, has two monsoons – the south-west (May to October) and the north-east (November–December).

80. Sunset from 'Chiriya-Tapu', the southernmost tip of South Andaman, with a large mangrove tree in the foreground.

23

"রূপসাগরে ডুব দিয়েছি অরূপ রতন আশা করি"

"I dive down into the depth of the ocean of forms,
hoping to gain the perfect pearl of the formless"

—Tagore

2

4

8

14

17

24

25

32

37

38

39

42

44

46

54

59

62

65

73

74